Fighting and Beating Depression

D1301441

Ronnie L. Worsham

ISBN: 148401751X
ISBN-13: 9781484017517

Cover by Matt Clark

dedication: To my faithful wife and dearest friend Tana, who has walked with me in the darkness through my "valley of the shadow of death," and never left my side.

TABLE OF CONTENTS

Chapter 1
Introduction

I have worked and strove for money,
Sought joy in excess,
And I have learned through all my searching,
That contentment is success!

I have worked with people extensively for nearly forty years now. Even before that, as the youngest of eight children, I had a ringside seat to struggles with depression as well as the whole panorama of emotional challenges. It ran in the family, although at the time I just thought it was a normal thing. Early on, I saw, heard, and learned of things that many people might not even see in their lifetimes. My dad suffered from bouts of depression, often accompanied intermittently by fits of rage. I had an uncle who was unmarried until he was in his forties, who had returned from World War II and lived with my grandparents. Looking back, I can see he suffered greatly from depression. I had an aunt who I am now sure was addicted to prescription sedatives because of her severe depression and anxiety. I have siblings who have suffered with it, as well.

On top of that, my wife and I have raised four children of our own, a couple of whom have had some mild issues with depression. It is an incredible, eye-opening, and enormously enlightening experience to have the honor of helping shape the lives of four special human beings. I consider the title "dad" to be my greatest honor, rivaled only by "husband."

Suffice it to say, I, along with anyone who works with people, have seen plenty of depression. It is so sad to see someone you love in a dark hole of depression. It's sort of like talking to my friends up North in the spring when it is beautiful here in Texas and it is still cold and cloudy there. I wish they could be in the sunshine with me. They do too! But there they are, stuck inside on a cold, cloudy, rainy, or snowy day. I can't give them what I have. They can't get rid of what they have.

A conversation with a depressed person can feel the same. Talking may make them feel better. Or talking may make them feel worse, though. Depression is complex, as those who study and write about it will attest. I am not writing this to assert that I am a specialist on the subject who has studied and researched depression extensively. I am not that and there are plenty of great resources available to those who want to learn more. Rather, I am writing as one who has in fact though studied it quite a bit, given spiritual counseling to many individuals who are dealing with it, and who has considerable experience with it in my own life.

I write this from the heart—from personal experience. I write it to "come alongside" those who might want to read an honest account of another's experiences. I certainly have been helped and strengthened by others' stories. I write to help people who love someone with depression to understand it better. I write it as one who has found the secret of contentment in life's most troubling situations, who has discovered the well of hope on the dark days and lonely nights of depression, and who has found the healing balms available from within, as well as from outside resources.

On another note, the poems at the beginnings of the chapters are my own. They are there to help me express the thoughts and feelings I write about in the chapter. Poetry often helps me get to the bottom of my melancholy emotions when I just cannot wrap my mind around them any other way. I have written poems my whole life but have only shared them more widely in recent years. Sharing my poems makes me feel very vulnerable, as most of them do indeed represent my deeper inner thoughts and emotions that often take me back emotionally, and sometimes painfully, to my childhood. Thus some you might note are written in simple, childlike words and rhymes.

Chapter 2
Personal Reflection on Depression
What the Heck Is It?

I have cried in the night for rescue,
Wept in the day for relief,
I have prayed that God would just take me,
Among the cursed, I've felt myself chief!

I have hopelessly wandered in darkness,
Listlessly mourned in dark grief,
Lain hours with my head in a pillow,
Had my joy stolen 'way by the Thief.

I've found the light at the end of the tunnel,
A lamp of hope on a cold, dark night,
Had my tears wiped away by his kind hand,
Found the strength to again stand aright.

Everyone who knows me well knows that I have had to face the specter of depression most of my life.

I've been pretty open about it, although most have never REALLY seen me depressed. Some might say I hide it or a counselor might suggest I repress it, but I prefer to think of it as sparing others my own personal darkness.

However because of it, I do relate to others who face bouts of depression. It is hard to even describe it to those who don't experience it. We often use the expression, "I struggle with depression," whatever that means. But, to say, "I'm depressed," is often inaccurate, as most of us aren't depressed all the time and many of us are pretty rarely in depression. So, what do we mean when we say we're "struggling" with depression?

Those who study and treat depression have lingo they use to describe and communicate about it, but socially we have struggled to find accurate descriptive language. Sadly, even Christians, who by definition have admitted that they are weak and imperfect, often have refused to be open about it and seek help, fearing shame and embarrassment. However, we are finally coming out of the closet with it. The shame previously so common with mental and emotional illness is finally starting to subside. We can talk about what goes on in our private worlds. And we can get help without embarrassment.

One of the biggest challenges faced by people who deal with depression is simply getting our minds around what it is. Is it a "bad mood"? Well, yeah, depression is a bad mood of sorts, but it is really not exactly that. Am I "in a funk"? Yeah, when you are depressed that description works, and for people who do not have chronic depression, it is probably descriptive enough. But for those who face bouts of depression on a regular basis, it is certainly more than a funk! Among those so inclined, depression can occur with varying frequency from every few years to multiple times in a day. There are also degrees of depression: from utter hopelessness to mild but troubling and persistent feelings and symptoms. There are also various facets of depression expressed in many combinations of possible symptoms.

For many of us, depression is simply something for which we have a propensity. Looking back, I can see the roots of my depression reaching back at least to when I was four. Depression is a type of underlying mindset that develops from within, above and beyond even our consciousness. It is our mental and emotional weather—our "inner climate." I wake up some mornings and it is just "cloudy." Not cloudy like having a hazy mind. I mean cloudy as in dreary and darker than normal. If others see it in me, they generally ask me if I'm upset. If I say, "I am just down a bit," they usually ask something like, "What are you upset about?" I'm left to ponder, of course. However, I have dealt with it pretty much my whole life, and my honest answer to that now is usually that I am upset with WHATEVER I think about when I am depressed. That is, if I am depressed, whatever I think about is darkened by the present mood. Depression is a dark lens through which I see the world at that moment.

There is indeed a situational type of depression that is triggered by tough life situations and disappointing events. Most everybody experiences it, and if they don't, that's likely another mental malady of its own. This kind of depression is just the normal emotional reaction to such pain. Some wouldn't even call it depression, although I think it is, in fact, a form of it. We are designed to feel sadness, loneliness, and a sense of loss. These are emotional reactions, and they will generally subside normally, although perhaps only gradually, just as the immediate pain of a banged knee will subside.

Chronic depression is different. It is like having the flu, and the whole body aches, is feverish, and is tired. When you are sick with the flu, every little thing that happens hurts so much more. The slightest physical effort can seem like too much. Depression is just that way emotionally. Little things hurt so much more that you do not want to try to do much other than hide or go to bed and try to not think about it until it goes away. Any exertion becomes stressful. (You might also feel in your heart like you are contagious; and I guess depression is in fact just a little bit contagious.) Depression is truly "mental and emotional illness." It generally is not like irrational mental illnesses, although it can become that. Rather, the kind of depression I am talking about is like the general malaise that comes with physical sickness. It is just that this malaise emerges from within us—from the mind and heart.

This kind of depression cannot just be "thought away" anymore than a cloudy day can be thought away. You cannot run outside on a gloomy day and wish the clouds away (unless you have the faith and prayer life of Elijah, of course, and most of us don't). You cannot go out with a giant electric fan and simply blow the clouds away. Most people who suffer with depression think that if they could "just think differently," it would go away. Outsiders also tend to think that way about those who are depressed. Do not get me wrong; good thinking is part of an effective strategy to get through and out of bouts of depression. However, "thinking rightly" is not a quick fix for the depressed; they are not just "feeling sorry" for themselves and in need of a quick pick-me-up.

Depression is to the experienced as snow is to Eskimos. In the course of doing research for a paper, my son once found that Eskimos have over twenty words to describe snow. Now, for us Oklahoma boys who maybe saw snow two or three times a year, snow was snow. And as a kid, with the infrequency with which we saw it, it was very good. But to a people who have lived and survived in snow their whole lives, there are all kinds of snow. Just saying "snow" is not descriptive enough for planning hunting trips or treacherous travel. It is the same with depression. As I said, there are all kinds and degrees of depression as well as types of moods associated with it. And I can assure you that they are not selected on a daily basis as we would select our clothes. We usually just get whatever falls from the emotional "weather" we are experiencing at that time. Everyone experiences mood fluctuations to some degree and thus can probably at least understand the underlying phenomenon.

So summarizing, the best way I can think of to understand depression is simply to think of it as a kind of mental and emotional weather. It is above and beyond us to a large degree, just like the weather is outside our control, even though depression and other moods are often triggered by events in our lives. We often wake up with it, unaware from whence it came. We can look out the window and see what sort of weather is up for the day. Similarly, those of us who suffer depression are looking into our own hearts to see what is up. In addition, just as the weather can change midday, we often experience emotional shifts midday. It can be dark and rainy for days. And it can be cloudy some days. It can be stormy and it can be hot or cold. It can be bright and sunny, as well. It can be sunny and then get cloudy or it can be cloudy and then get sunny. All kinds of combinations are possible. And the swings themselves make one feel crazy and out of control.

The reality is that everyone has mental weather. It is just that some people are like the Arizona desert: they wake up "sunny" most every day. For them, a cloudy, rainy day is pretty mild, just like a cloudy, rainy day in the desert is completely unimpressive to someone from Portland or Seattle. I remember when I lived in Arizona hearing someone comment on a fairly light rain, saying, "It's pouring down rain out there." Being accustomed to the torrential downpours of thunderstorms in Oklahoma, I looked out and almost laughed at the thought. It seemed to be barely raining at all! It is all a matter of perspective.

But for those who face chronic bouts of depression, getting a perspective on it is one of the greatest and most important challenges. For those who do not experience it, it is probably still just as important for them to get the right perspective on depression lest their judgments and reactions hurt others they love, and as well damage their ability to be a help and support.

Chapter 3
My Early Experiences

A little boy's picture hangs on the wall
In the back of my older man's mind;
Its frame is tarnished with sadness,
The faint smile seems sadder with time.

Having been a minister for over thirty-five years, I have had plenty of cause to examine my own past experiences as I examine others' experiences during counseling and mentoring. Hence, I've analyzed and reanalyzed and surely over-analyzed my past. I do have some pretty deep and extensive memories of my emotional experiences from very early on, so there is plenty to think on.

I actually have some "snapshot" memories from when I was two years old. (I have a vague memory of taking a bath in the kitchen sink one time.) My family swears this cannot be true, but I just know it is. I have quite a few short, "video-clip" memories of when I was three and four. I have some pretty extensive short "movie" memories of when I was five and beyond. I even have memories of moods associated with most of them. The fact that I noticed them at such an early age and remember them tells me there has always been some significance to my moods.

I can still get in touch with some of these feelings I felt very early on. In remembering them, I can feel again what I felt then. For instance, with the bath, I was embarrassed that a young woman from next door bathed me. Oddly, I'm not what most people would consider an overly emotional type of person, either. Obviously, though, I was indeed emotionally impressionable—I still am. I am also one who has always been in touch with my feelings. Sometimes I feel that is unfortunate; other times it is quite a blessing!

My first memory of real depression was when I was six. A teacher had told a little girl and me that we were going to have a very special part in the first-grade play. I was honored and excited. I remember walking on the playground at recess feeling really good and anticipating the honor associated with it. Then, all of a sudden, it went mentally sour for me. It was a profound experience because I could not get the positive feeling of anticipation back. I developed this sense of dread or mental "darkness" that I could not shake. It really bothered me. I was sad about it for at least a week. On top of that, the plans changed and I did not even get to do it at all! It is hard to know what kicked in that day, but it was the beginning of a whole chain of experiences I believe were associated.

What I do know is that soon I began to have strong bouts of dysphoria on a regular basis. I could not experience—or would not let myself experience—good feelings for any length of time. Dysphoria is a term used in psychology and is basically the opposite of euphoria. It describes a general feeling or mood of anxiety, discomfort, or despondency. If I did cut loose and let myself experience the good feelings, they would quickly turn sad within me, becoming instead a sense of dread and despondency. And the saddest part was that from then on, when I would think about an upcoming experience or event that should be enjoyable, the sadness stayed connected to it so that I had trouble even enjoying the event itself. So, when something I truly looked forward to, like Christmas, drew near, I would try not to think about it lest it get "tainted" by the monster that lurked in my inner thoughts. I still find myself doing the same thing—not allowing myself to think about things I might otherwise look forward to.

Another odd mental experience soon emerged. I began to develop an aversion to various individuals. The experience was similar to the feeling I mentioned above, however, it was associated with certain people under particular circumstances. It would occur when I was with somebody, or even just thinking about somebody, I really liked and to whom I felt close. Then without warning a sense of dread and despondency about the person would come over me. I would develop a strong aversion to that person; I would feel sort of sick around him or her. Sometimes the dread was stronger than at other times, but when it happened, I would just stay away from that person to avoid the bad feelings. If I was with the person when it happened, I just wanted to run away—and often did, without explanation.

The first time it happened was with a little girl who I really liked. She was my girlfriend. One day something snapped and I had a strong aversion to her. Nothing happened to cause it, although in our family system, cherished things and events often were taken away for no apparent reason, or we could be teased and humiliated over something seemingly innocuous. But this dread came from within. I certainly didn't understand it then, and still don't, really. She didn't understand it either. She wanted to walk with me to the bus after school that day and I simply told her that I had to hurry and began running to the bus. She ran beside me. I ran faster. I don't think I even said good-bye to her. That was it. It would be a funny kid story, except it signaled a demon developing inside of me. It was a sort of dysphoria about people. And once it developed toward someone, it did not soon go away or did not go away at all. This happened with a girl I dated in college.

So when I would spend time with a friend or a teacher and start to have good feelings about him or her, I would try to distance myself immediately and not think about those warm feelings lest the aversion hit. It was not as strong with my immediate family, but there were pangs of it even with them. Into adulthood, this malady alienated me greatly from certain people, especially people with whom I might have otherwise connected.

So there I was, detaching myself from anticipatory thoughts as well as from individuals who might otherwise make me feel happy or important. You can imagine the fears and anxieties that were developing within me. And you can probably imagine the sense of inner isolation that was developing as I detached myself from people to whom I was attracted. Not because I did not want to be around them, but because I DID want to be around them. In order for me to have the sense of closeness to people that I so desperately wanted, I began to avoid getting too close to anyone lest the aversion develop. I would try to get close and then back off and hold the other person at arm's length.

Without going into detail, there were plenty of triggering events in my home. Certainly, my mom becoming seriously ill with heart disease when I was just starting school and then dying just before my twelfth birthday had a profound impact on me as well as on my whole family system. Only later could I see that I was living with a father who was often deeply depressed and who most assuredly had some associated personality disorders. So yes, there is clearly an inherited factor working within me. Also, there were the obvious and subsequent social and emotional effects of living with a depressed father—the classic double whammy of genetics and socialization gone awry. The whole family system was emotionally awry. We were all generally depressed for a long time, I think.

Chapter 4
More Experiences

I have cried in the day for the nighttime,
I have wept in the night for the day,
A boy stuck in despair and confusion,
Without joy or the simple will to play.

As early as the first grade, I remember lying in bed in this melancholy state, experiencing mild to extreme despondency. I had already developed erratic sleep patterns and would lie awake late or wake up in the middle of the night alert and scared. It was NOT okay to wake up anybody in our house at night, so I would just lie there in my dark thoughts. During those years, I first experienced the desire to go to sleep and not wake up. Those feelings later became full-blown suicidal thoughts. I experienced self-loathing. I resented my father for his meanness. He was the son of an alcoholic and battled his own depression and rage. I resented my brothers and sisters for their constant teasing and harassment. I have four brothers and three sisters, ranging up to fifteen years older than I. Thus, in my early years, counting my parents, there were ten of us packed into the very close quarters of a small, three-bedroom house. Later a fourth small bedroom was added. There was little chance of privacy or protection. Our dad put in place a system of inter-sibling discipline based on teasing. We learned to be cruel to each other by "joking." My dad was the "referee" when he was around and he believed it was good for us. It was hard on all of us, to various degrees.

I felt unsafe and scared most of the time. I hated life. However, I had to act happy around my dad, as it was not okay to be depressed. If I let it show, I was accused of pouting and being a big baby. That was his way of "getting me out of it."

During those years, I developed the fantasy of a safe-box I could get into whenever I wanted. It was cozy and had whatever I wanted in it. It was climate-controlled—cool in the summer and warm in the winter. It was soft and fur-lined. It was completely safe. For goodness sakes, it locked from the inside! No one else could get in. I would fantasize all sorts of protective and self-serving designs for it based on my then current feelings of sadness, fear, discomfort, etc. This fantasy went on well into my adolescence.

After my mom died, I also invented an alter ego—a person who was a super-human kind of guy. For reasons unknown even to me, I gave him the name Bill McKenzie. I don't like to be teased about this name because it is associated with so much pain. Bill McKenzie was everything I did not feel I was. I would become him on a moment's notice. Along with my mental box, he was an escape when I needed one. He was a great teacher. He was a great athlete. He was masculine. He was strong. He was a professional basketball player, an Olympic gymnast or an acrobat or a scientist. He was independent. He was happy. He was free. He certainly wasn't depressed. Bill McKenzie was whatever I "needed" him to be at the time. I have heard similar stories from others. Some play-acting is normal and healthy for kids. However, this was beyond healthy, in my estimation. Bill McKenzie stayed with me well into college in at least some subtle ways. But no one knew him or even knew about him back then, but over the years I have told a few friends and family about him. Just like my box, he was another escape from a painful reality. He was my safety valve—my strong, independent dream. I would become him when I felt weak or wanted to feel good about myself.

There was a parallel development. I was becoming emotionally detached from others and completely independent emotionally. I worked very hard to not depend on anybody. This built up over the years until my sophomore year in college, when I withdrew and began to spend most of my time by myself. I was pretty miserable that year. I could not stand to depend on anybody for anything, physically or emotionally. I had mostly made my own way through college through government assistance, scholarships, and work, but that year I stopped taking any money from my dad. Prior to that, he would give me five or ten dollars if I went home for a weekend. But the emotional cost of taking that money became too high for me. The cost was loss of control, spoken and unspoken abasement, and constant badgering. For some reason, he seemed to need to "break" the people around him. My best guess is that he did it to feel in control of his own life. He grew up working on the family farm during the extremely hard years of the Great Depression and Dust Bowl, and was himself the son of a hopeless alcoholic.

The summer before my junior year in college, I moved into a two-bedroom apartment by myself. I further withdrew from people. I also withdrew completely from God. We had been a part of a small conservative church growing up, but I have little memory of it after the death of my mother just before I turned twelve. Plus, there was little emphasis on any personal relationship with God anyway. In fact, at that point I lost any real belief in God at all. I was completely alone and independent. Detached, really. I remember one of my fellow chemistry majors saying in a lab one day, "What do you do outside of school? Nobody really knows you or anything about you." That described it pretty well. I didn't understand it at all, and I don't think others, even my family, knew I was very depressed.

Depression dogged me over the years. It was not a constant companion, but it was a regular visitor. Often, extreme fatigue seemed to trigger it. With my erratic sleep pattern, hard work ethic, and my love for staying up late, I got exhausted regularly. I called it "hitting the wall." Protracted feelings of frustration were another trigger. Dealing with personal failure and shortcomings were also key triggers. I had unwittingly been programmed through constant teasing, criticism, and ridicule to feel fat, stupid, and ugly. I never felt that I pleased others, even though I desperately wanted to do so.

My reaction was to be an over-achiever. My mom died the July before I went into the seventh grade. School started in August. Going back to school brought on another tsunami of reality having to go back home to that sad, lonely house. One day early in the school year, right after lunch, I was sitting by myself in a swing on the playground. I remember feeling awful and sad. All life and energy seemingly had drained from me. So when the bell rang for class, I couldn't get up. I was frozen solid, so to speak. I had always been pretty good about following rules (probably mainly because I feared my dad's wrath), but I just couldn't make myself get out of the swing and go inside. I literally felt paralyzed. I remember one of my friends running by and saying it was time to go in. I just ignored him; didn't even reply. I just stayed there.

It is a surreal recollection. I have vivid memories of what I saw and felt. I do not know how long I stayed out there before the elementary school principal came to get me. He also served as the quasi-guidance counselor for graduating seniors trying to go to college. I guess somebody told him that I was just sitting out there. It was a small school, so he knew me well. He'd been my teacher in the sixth grade. I had no clue that everyone at school knew we had lost our mom. I certainly had no sense that anybody at school would care. Oddly, I never talked much to my friends about home. I probably was protecting embarrassing secrets. Anyway, the principal just came out and said, "Ronnie, it's time to go to class." I suppose I thought I would get in big trouble as we walked quietly across the playground toward the building.

As we approached the glass doors and I saw his and my reflections, I thought to myself that I would just make straight A's that year. Odd thought, huh? Our minds work that way. I had always been a good student and school was pretty easy for me. I had never even tried to make straight A's though, as A's and B's were good enough, and easy to make. This was my first manic moment, as far as I can recall. The thought made me feel powerful and in control of something. It gave me something to aim for and to be proud of. The challenge gave me some sense purpose I guess. It was the beginning of an over-achiever syndrome of sorts. I call it a "manic moment" because I have observed that such moments have long been one of my ways out of depression. I have actually learned to conjure them at times in order to get myself going. They would not likely be classified diagnostically as manic episodes, but it is still the best way I can describe them and they definitely have that leaning. I have mostly experienced them during times when I was depressed. In them I feel powerful, hopeful and motivated. I make bold commitments to myself and commit myself to achievement, such as I just mentioned, making straight A's in school. And while I have experienced mild bipolar type episodes over the years, the truly irrational phases were always the depressive ones not really the corresponding manic feelings. Depression was by far my main issue.

By the way, I did not get into trouble that day, as he signed a pass for me and I just went to class and sat down. Nobody ever said another word about it, and I just stored the whole experience away. No one dared call my dad, I suppose. Those were days when counseling and emotional support were fairly non-existent, especially out in the rural areas. You did not tell anybody your problems. You survived and fought on, mainly alone. In fact, telling others could actually cause you more trouble and compound the problem. I wonder sometimes if the whole incident might have been a subconscious way for me to cry out for help and support.

In various ways, relationship issues also triggered depression. Remembering some of my extremely self-destructive thoughts, I think I was on the cusp several times of taking a tragic emotional downturn. Although I was not personally "with" God, I would come to see later that God was with me through all this and saved me in spite of myself. I then developed another alter ego that I would lapse into. However, unlike Bill McKenzie, this person was not powerful and independent but rather was pained and detached, and of course, depressed. I certainly was unaware of what was happening at the time.

My wife would later tell my counselor that my facial expressions and mannerisms changed when I became this other. I realized later that he even had a first name, which I have never disclosed to anyone else. So, I now had an alter ego to express my manic, over-achiever self as well as one to express my depressed self. These personalities were real, intense, and entrenched within me.

One of the things I remembered in counseling was that when I was five and six, I went through a phase of putting my head in the toilet. I did not ever go so far as to put it in the water, but I would put my head inside and let the cover rest on my head. I did some other funky things like that I do not even want to share. Sad. I have heard many stories of the odd and even destructive things others did in childhood. I have tried over the years to understand what I was getting out of that or what I was achieving. I think what I felt then is fairly obvious, though. It was during a time when I was trying desperately to gain favor with those around me and I felt I was of little value to anybody—except to my mom. In hindsight, I realize that my emotional detachment kept me from internalizing the love and encouragement that was actually there, even though at times it was quite meager.

Often in response to despondency, I would throw myself on the couch, put my face in the crack between pillows, and stay there until somebody made me stop. I can remember not being able to breathe and not caring. In adolescence, I began to get into bed and put the pillow over my head. When I had to breathe I would raise the pillow up just high enough to inhale. When depression struck, I would get there just as quickly as possible. I withdrew and I hid. I was on emotional overload and I needed to be in a safe place where there were no burdens or negative emotional stimulation. Of course, after I got married, my poor wife wondered what she'd gotten herself into.

I first went for professional counseling when I was about twenty-three. I was terrified, but I was also desperate. I had a ton of baggage. I was ashamed to have to seek counseling and except for my wife-to-be, I told no one. I finally reached out to a wonderful elder in the church I attended in the town where I was a student. He was the first person I had really ever spoken to about all my inner struggles. It was he who set me up with a therapist. The counseling really wasn't all that great, but it was a start. When I moved to Texas in 1989 at the age of thirty-seven, I took the opportunity to find a counselor who was a good fit for me, and I aggressively proceeded to try to put my life into perspective. I saw the counselor for over a year. A few years later, I went through another year or so of counseling with another therapist. These were the first times I had found others who understood me and understood the kinds of things I had been through. With God's help, I got myself better in a lot of ways. For the most part, I left my alter egos behind, and I began to think clearly about what was going on. Indeed, I left some pretty self-destructive thoughts and behaviors behind. Yes, I still got depressed, but while I was emotionally ill during those times, I did not have to be mentally ill, too!

I escaped depression for a few years in the late 1990s but after a nephew's protracted battle with cancer and subsequent death in January 2000, depression swept over me again. This particular nephew had been born to my sister out of wedlock. This sister had left home a mess. My dad seemingly disliked her and mistreated her, and she grew to live in a fantasy world all her own. She was thus a trained victim for the predatory older guy who got her pregnant. Thank God she did not marry him! But her son was a sweet, innocent, little guy. He seems to have been such a metaphor for our whole family's life.

I had become a surrogate father figure to him and remained so over the years. I took care of him quite a bit early on. When I was eighteen and he was around two, he asked me if I would be his daddy. I had to turn my face so he wouldn't see me crying. I felt so sorry for him, as my sister was so often depressed, lonely, and just generally unhappy. She worked the midnight shift and was usually sleep-deprived and exhausted, and with her depression, she just wanted to sleep her life away. Despite all of her struggles, though, she was a dedicated and faithful mom and she loved him dearly.

As best as I can understand, his pain and death brought back my feelings of utter helplessness. Several times when I sat with him and held his frail body on the night he died, he looked at me with wild, pained eyes, and shouted, "It hurts!" By that time, I couldn't tell if he even clearly recognized me, although I think he did. He was in such bitter agony. The cancer had started in his colon when he was only twenty-five. He underwent colon surgery, radiation, and chemotherapy. He had a few years of relative health before the cancer appeared in his kidneys and spine. Those who have watched someone die of cancer know the routine. He withered away. The week before he died, he was still talking about what he could do to live on. During the interim between his bouts of cancer, he had had a little girl out of wedlock. He adored her and wanted desperately to take care of her. A day or two before he died, he asked me if I thought he was a candidate for a kidney transplant! It was horrible. I had always tried to solve problems for him and help out however I could. I was utterly helpless and felt like I had failed him somehow. I felt as though I had failed my sister, too.

He died in the middle of the night with his mom, our closest brother, and me sitting by him on the bed. Words can't describe the pain of such moments. His mom had depended on me a lot through the years. We shared the bond of survival we had developed in childhood. As badly as I felt, I could not even imagine what she was feeling. My psyche took a real beating. The subsequent depression was deep and dark and it came on suddenly and unexpectedly.

Few people knew about my depression, though. I preferred to bleed in secret with a pillow over my head, at least figuratively—and literally, when possible. I had learned well how to hide it growing up. I was married to a beautiful woman. I had four wonderful children. I was a successful minister in my dream church, in which I was the founding pastor and leader. I was a successful management consultant and leadership trainer who taught others how to live and be productive at work. I knew many of the answers and was considered wise and knowledgeable by those that sought me out. However, most did not yet know about the hours of counseling I had undergone in an effort to "get my head on straight." After all, I was the one who was helping everyone else get better. Right? The guy who helped others was once again fighting for his own peace and even his sanity.

Chapter 5
Later Experiences

How Great Thou Art,
Amazing Grace,
Rock of Ages,
Beholding God's Face!

In 2004, my mentee became my mentor. But first, some additional background is necessary. In 1992, I had reluctantly gone back into part-time vocational ministry, training leaders and developing small groups in a larger church. In 1997, a few other families and individuals, along with my family started a nondenominational church nearby. I had been in vocational ministry from 1976 to 1988, but had left it, determining to go a completely different direction, but returned by what I felt to be a strong calling from God. Many saw the formation of the new church as a church-split, and to some degree it was, though quite unintentionally. But in spite of all of our shortcomings, shortsightedness, and possibly even sin, forming the new church was truly an act of God—a God-deal. That's our web address, Goddeal.com. I have been the senior minister ever since.

I have been involved in leadership training throughout my career. I completed a master's degree in business administration in 1991 and started my own management consulting company, which I operate to this day. Since 1992, I have worked in secular training and consulting with business leaders and employees, and I also have served simultaneously in ministry. Since 1997, I have been the senior minister of a church dedicated to starting new churches and building campus ministries, using Biblical, personalized, but not-necessarily-traditional approaches. My two parallel careers, which involve working extensively with people from all walks, have afforded me extraordinary opportunities to learn about people in all of their life roles and arenas. Daily, I see people "up close and personal," to say the least. From my vantage point I see and hear about lives "from bedroom to boardroom."

The man who became our youth minister was a person I had served with, mentored, and developed in ministry almost from the beginning of the founding of our church. Through our work together, he truly had become one of the dearest and most faithful friends I'd ever had. He managed to win my trust and get inside my heart without me developing any aversion and having to hide. As with my wife, I could not "hide" from him. He cared enough to want to know me at a time that I was desperate, in a way. The timing was right and the Spirit led me to let this very young man become my crutch. He still is today. He is my Timothy. In the course of training and developing him in ministry, I ultimately shared my whole story. Against my better judgment due to his youthfulness, I allowed him became my chief sounding board and confidant. I began to regularly let him see through my outer façade into my heart when it was the most pained.

For years I had thought about trying antidepressant medication along with my other strategies. Others had suggested it more than once. My wife, who deserves an award for valor and patience, had encouraged me to try them on and off for years. My medical doctor at the time, and also a trusted friend and godly brother, had spoken to me about them during my annual physicals, but I quickly fended him off.

However, even with all my education and experience, I was woefully ignorant of how they worked. In addition, I have always taken my example as a minister very seriously and thus have always been cautious about what I do. I must admit that I was also concerned about health and life insurance! Sadly, in the past, companies either charged you much higher rates or refused to insure you at all if you ever had taken antidepressants. I understand why, but this is still unfortunate.

Further, as I mentioned earlier, as I child I had an aunt who obviously struggled with depression and anxiety and took sedatives that caused her to act "punch-drunk" much of the time. (Yeah, punch-drunk is an old boxing expression, but it is by far the best description I can think of.) I guess I may have had visions of that. Furthermore, I had a counselor friend who had misgivings about antidepressants and shared some thoughts that deterred me from using them. One day when I was fighting a serious bout of depression, my young friend looked me in the eyes and simply told me I ought to at least try them. His understated style of suggestion, and the fact that I knew he sincerely loved and believed in me, prevailed over my reservations. I set up an appointment with my doctor. When I went in, he did a depression workup on me and said I was clearly clinically depressed. (Surprise! Surprise!) He prescribed Wellbutrin. He told me it would take at least a couple of weeks to take hold.

However, within the first week something dramatic began to happen within me. In all honesty, I was not expecting much from the medicine. I have never been one who likes to take medications, and I generally have low expectations when I take them. However to my surprise, although the effect came on subtly at first, it came on profoundly in a short time. Previously, I had often felt as if I was walking along the edge of a cliff and one misstep could cause me to plunge into a dark canyon below. But after taking the medication for just a few days, I started to feel farther and farther away from the edge. Much safer. The edge was still in sight, but I found I had the strength to fight off depression as various triggers occurred. The small dose I was taking did not shut down feelings of sadness or remorse over the things that would normally bother me, but I just felt more normal. The dark clouds no longer formed in my head. I was able to deal with life's issues straight up rather than having to fight through them in the darkness of depression. I stopped slipping into depression. I felt I could breathe again. Honestly, I was quite amazed by the drug's benefits.

One note I must make here is that antidepressant medication is not an elixir. And it is not even an answer for everybody who deals with depression. Medication needs to be only a part of the overall strategy for those that it helps. Such medications need to be tried under close medical supervision, and, I believe, in conjunction with a trustworthy counselor. Do not trust encouragers or detractors who are not professionals. In fact, do not trust those who push any medication or supplement as the cure-all, either. I practice what I preach in all of this. Antidepressants do not work well for everyone. Antidepressants often come with unpleasant side effects. Not everyone has the positive experiences that I have had, for sure. But it is a worthwhile strategy for many.

Concurrent to all of this was the spiritual side of my life journey. My mom had become a committed Christian when I was a small boy. She took us to church regularly before she died all too soon. We had a very strong moral education when I was young, although we dealt with many inconsistencies and contradictions. I was baptized when I was nine or ten. I remember that the night I was baptized, she came in to the room I shared with my brother and read something to us. She had tried to read it to us in the living room, but my dad was trying to watch television and made her stop. It was really an act of defiance and pretty risky for her to take us back into our room and continue reading. I realized that at the time, and it meant a lot to me. It is truly one of the later and best memories I have of my mom. I really do not remember her reading to me very often as I was growing up, but I do remember the deep feeling of joy I had in that moment—the profound feeling that my mom was proud of me. I certainly enjoyed the attention that night. She had always been a great mother though as far as I was concerned.

After she died, our Christianity waned, although our dad did keep up his insistence on "perfect" behavior. He was so very demanding. In the long run, the upside to that has actually served me well in life. The downside to it is a whole other story! There were four of us still living at home when my mom died. Being the youngest, I sadly and painfully had to watch each of the other three leave home for college. I loved my family dearly and knew they loved me. But we had a very conflicted family system. We were trained and controlled with embarrassment and even humiliation. I cannot describe the utter hopelessness I felt the day that my brother, to whom I was so close in age and size that we were treated like twins, left for college two hours away. He was my best friend and buddy. We were seldom allowed to invite our friends to the house, so this particular brother and I became very close. When he left, I was alone with my dad and was so bitterly sad and lonely. My only consoling thought was that I would be able to leave in one year. Although I did not understand it at the time, I was severely depressed.

That last year at home was cruel at times and pretty bad for me all the time. I fell into a prolonged period of off-and-on-again depression. My dad had worked extremely hard on the farm and then in the oil-field. As a man, he would not do housework—he had grown up in an era when men simply did not do that work. However, it was okay for me and he forced me to do it. You can see how that left me feeling. Because I was a sensitive kid, he had teased me and called me a sissy much of my life anyway. I had tried extra hard to prove my manhood in the midst of an alpha male system where I had a dominant father and four older brothers. Then, to be dominated by three sisters only added to the challenge of any kind of healthy personal growth and development.

After mom died, dad repeatedly told the four of us left at home that if we wanted to make a home, we would have to do all the housework because he would not. Otherwise, we would have to find another place to live. I was terrified at first at the prospect and then later I was numb to it.

Right after she died, when we were all in the hospital room with her dead body still lying as it had in those last hours, I cried and screamed, asking who was going to take care of me. My dad clearly indicated over the coming days, months, and years that he did not want that role. The first time he said it, we were sitting in the car in front of the hospital waiting for the undertaker to come take her body. Dad's job would be to work and he would just be boss. That's the way it went. So, when my brother left, I was a seventeen-year-old boy (actually, sixteen when he drove off) who was completely in charge of cooking and cleaning and paying bills! I am not exaggerating one bit. And I was alone, dealing daily with a deeply depressed, mentally ill, and demanding father. It was a nightmare.

In my senior year of high school, I also drove a school bus since we lived at the end of a route in a rural school district. To save money, our little country school system sent some of us students to a bus-driver training school so we could drive the buses to save on gasoline expenses. I was excited about the money and knew I could help my sister, who was pregnant and in trouble. However, sadly, Dad made me put my check into his checking account, on which only he could write checks. It was just one more nail in my emotional coffin at the time.

In all of this, I did not know how to turn to God, and I sure did not feel close to him. I did not know how to turn to anybody. On top of that, I had people aversions. The church we had gone to did not really even teach about developing a personal relationship to God anyway, and country schools did a little bit of guidance and no counseling. I do not remember anything about church through high school, so I assume we just never went. Dad had never gone to church with us so it was up to us to get up and go. After my sisters left, I do not think my brother and I went anymore. Needless to say, I just lived to survive that year. I never could fully describe what I went through. I was awfully bitter, often depressed, and fantasized about suicide with regularity. Conversely, as a deflection, and perhaps for survival, I was also a class clown, laughing on the outside but crying on the inside.

When I went to college, what little was left of my weak, simple, childhood faith and conversion was no match for college life and my study of science and psychology. I developed very serious doubts, and those doubts, stirred in with my unresolved pain, destroyed my faith. As the story commonly goes for so many, it was hard to believe in a God who would let us go through such pain. There were too many questions I could not reconcile with the simplistic and sorely insufficient teaching (at least for me) I had grown up with. This dark world is good at obscuring the wonderful truth of the one true God and the incredibly good news of Jesus Christ.

At the start of my junior year in college, I was coming off another very dark year. I had mostly stayed to myself and hidden most of my feelings. Guys didn't discuss feelings much anyway. I did not want to have another miserable year like the one I had just experienced, though. I got a much better job working in a lab. I was getting a degree in chemistry, and this job was a real reward for me. I more than doubled my previous minimum wage salary and was able to move into an apartment by myself. Because of the emotional and spiritual storm I was in, and for a number of other reasons, I decided to look into the Bible and church. Actually, my search was set in motion when my physical chemistry teacher, who I later learned was a Christian, mentioned the scientific feasibility of an omnipresent being like the God of the Bible. It piqued my interest in God, and led me to act.

A month or so later I started going to church. My brother was going to church with his girlfriend, now his wife of forty years, and I decided to go with them. During that time I borrowed a Bible from her parents and started reading. Initially, my reading and experiences with church only exacerbated my doubt and unbelief. However, eventually my involvement with the small campus ministry, a real friendship with a truly Christian guy, and my reading and study started building a real faith. I was saved in the fall of 1973. As far as getting involved in church, it did not hurt that my brother's mother-in-law-to-be was an awesome cook and would often invite me to huge and incredibly good Sunday lunches! Just being in a home environment with a mom was, I think, an important part of my conversion and early growth. God is always working and knows what he is doing!

In the church community, I found the foundational pieces to the puzzle that my life had become. The preacher at the church profoundly influenced me, even though at first I mostly admired him from a distance. I was deeply moved by the love and guidance of one of the elders in particular. Later, two other elders had a significant influence on me. Quite a few other individuals played roles, as well. I developed the first true friends I had ever really dared to have, even though I was still secretly battling the people-aversion issue. I felt sorry for many of the people who had tried to befriend me before. I know I was not a good friend. I didn't know how to be, and I was so emotionally messed up.

However now, I was finding real answers in the Bible and a worthwhile purpose for living. I first developed a logical belief in God through the study of Christian evidences and apologetics. That one could correlate science and faith was an incredible discovery to me. I needed to see science, logic, and history reconciled with the faith of the Bible. It happened gradually. I was prepared to walk away from it all if I could not come to believe it. I did come to a belief in God, though partly because I could NOT believe what I had to believe to believe it all just happened. There were sound Biblical reasons to believe, internal and external to the Bible itself. I figured out that whatever I ended up believing about origins and such would prove to be "unbelievable" anyway. Living and working in a world of science and logic, I came to see that everyone lived by faith—in something. As far as I was concerned, there was lots of faith in academia and much of it even blind and closed-minded. I have never since been intimidated by academic and often arrogant attacks on faith!

After developing an intellectual belief, I came to believe in my heart that Jesus was the one he claimed to be. So much of this was nurtured through the church family that surrounded me. But this also happened unexpectedly through an incidental meeting and the surprising effect of a preacher I heard at a Christian conference and then visited personally with for a few minutes. He was the kind of man I pictured Christ being. For me, he was able to bring it all together and make it real. It didn't hurt that I found out he had a chemistry degree. I fully believed and was baptized into Christ that week in September 1973.

In faith, I discovered the path to my own healing and purpose. I found the powerful words from God to be true: "We have this hope as an anchor for the soul, firm and secure" (Heb. 6:19). In my Christian walk, I had a whole new battle to fight. Before, I was fighting simply for my own happiness through human efforts. It had yielded some results but those efforts ultimately were powerless against the deeper issues and forces involved. In Christ, I found the real battlefield—the battlefield of my mind and heart. I found it to be true that,

> Our struggle is not against flesh and blood, but against the rulers, against the authorities, against the powers of this dark world and against the spiritual forces of evil in the heavenly realms (Eph. 6:12).

Yes, the world had dealt its blows. Yes, I was often my own worst enemy. But through Christ, I found out who the real enemy was, and it was not others and it was not me.

When I figured that out, I could begin fighting the real battle. And in Christ I found the only way for me to truly win that battle. I found that the one who is living in us, the Holy Spirit of God, is much greater than the one who rules this present dark world (1 John 4:4).

It was during these spiritually formative years that I completed a master's degree in behavioral studies in the natural sciences. It was an education-oriented degree that allowed me to take half my classes in my major field of the natural sciences and the other half in psychology and education. I had also completed an undergraduate minor in education, which afforded me the opportunity to study quite a bit of psychology as an undergrad. So, between my two degrees, I basically had the equivalent of a degree in psychology. The convergence of my Christian experience with my psychology studies helped me begin to understand the psychological demons within me—first and foremost depression. It would still be over ten years before I really got a handle on just how serious and severe an issue it had been and still was for me.

Chapter 6
My Melancholy Personality

Working and climbing—achieving,
Thinking and mulling without end,
Burning the candle from both ends,
Wearing myself out from within.

One of the things I've been most intrigued by educationally, spiritually, vocationally, and personally are temperaments and personality styles. Some people love and study things like cars, guns, stamps, sports, etc. As for me, I just love people. I observe and know their types and styles just as car aficionados know cars. There are all kinds of theories and approaches to the human subject. There are all sorts of ways specialists in the field "slice and dice" human behavior and psychology to describe us. I do not consider myself a researcher or a psychologist, but I do consider myself an experienced practitioner, after working with people of all kinds and ages for nearly forty years. One thing I have learned is that it is paramount for each of us to come to understand ourselves if we are to deal effectively with our depression.

With that said, I can tell you that I am a "thinker" and I am a "doer." There are different descriptions for these, such as the four humors of Greco-Roman medicine—choleric, melancholy, sanguine, and phlegmatic. Tons of material has been written about this if you care to do some research. In this regard, my personality would be considered primarily melancholy and choleric. It's the melancholy side that houses my depression, although my choleric side provides plenty of fuel for the flames.

I believe that your greatest strengths are also your greatest weaknesses. In an ironic way, the inverse is true too—your greatest weaknesses are your greatest strengths. Now, you may not use them that way, of course. It is like the heads and tails on a coin. You cannot throw away one without throwing away the other. Get-things-done people will also be impatient people. On the other hand, impatient people are the ones who tend to get things done—usually while everyone else is waiting for "something" or for "someone," and often when no one knows what or whom! So there are relative strengths and weaknesses with each type of personality or temperament as it applies to life's challenges and needs. None is inherently negative or positive, but only negative or positive based on certain situations and what we do with our personalities.

The melancholy side of me is the part that makes me thoughtful, analytical, and emotional. It also leads me to be withdrawn and introspective—a thinker. I actually have an introverted side to my personality, although because of my positions, most people never really see it. The choleric part of me is my driver. I like to be active and need to accomplish things. I can be obsessive and compulsive. I can be a perfectionist. Basically, I struggle with many of the classic weaknesses of the choleric-melancholy personality. I also enjoy the basic strengths, though.

Being so thoughtful and sensitive in a big, clamorous, and sometimes dysfunctional family was a toxic mix for me as a child, however. There were ample opportunities to get my feelings hurt, feel put down, get rejected, and experience other things that a child simply cannot properly understand. Being a choleric-driver sort pushed me to be assertive and to get involved, often to my own detriment. Needless to say, I opened my mouth when I would have been better off saying nothing. I got myself in trouble by asking the wrong questions or making "unacceptable" comments, while some of my quieter, older, and probably smarter, siblings stayed out of firing range.

But my mind would just churn and race. I would walk around thinking about stuff that little children should not be thinking about. As with young people who suffer various abuses, I knew things I should not really have known. I am very curious about life, and I have always been an acquirer of lots of information about the humankind. I wondered why my dad was always so angry and seemingly just mean. I wondered what my mom thought about things, as she was very quiet and reserved in my presence, but still she always seemed so sad underneath it all. I wondered why my older brothers and sisters loved to laugh at me (and each other) so much—teasing and embarrassing me constantly. I wondered if others outside our family heard, saw, and did the things that we did. I wondered what was normal. I remember at least a few times lying awake late at night and hearing my dad berating my mom. I battled against hating him. I remember suffering great anxiety about the possibility of her dying; even before we found out she was ill. And I was scared out of my wits so much of the time. My family loved to scare one another, and I caught it all. I still have tremendous sleep problems, some of which, I'm sure, stem from these early years. And my mind still churns and races.

Being a choleric, driver, doer type, I need to get things done. I've been a lifelong student, as you can tell from my resume. Anyone who has ever played sports with me knows that I am a relentless competitor; even if I am playing something that I am not good at (and I am certainly no professional at anything). Just as I had to clean my room and apartment before I could study, I have to tidy up my office and even my house in order to do work. Then I look it all over as I walk through and enjoy the tidiness of it! I sometimes write things I have already done on my "To Do" list so that I can check them off! And don't judge me; I know a lot of others do stuff just as crazy. Remember, I do lots of counseling, so I know that we all can be just a little bit crazy.

But I have accepted myself as I am. Honestly, I do believe that the first step to true growth and change is to be able to understand who you are and to accept yourself. It is as with a car—know the make, model, and makeup of it; know what the engine can and cannot do; know about the transmission; know how well-built it really is; know if you can "get on it" or not; kick the tires; slam the doors; look under the hood, etc. You know. It took me far too long to do this. Like so many, I was afraid of the truth. But I found out that fear was the worst enemy of all. Most of my life, I felt I had to "be" a certain person at various times, and thus I had to reject who I really was in order to be this "expected" one. I am a pretty good style-flexer (adjusting one's own style to communicate with and effectively inter- act with others). But acting differently than our core being creates inherent stress in us, just as bending a bamboo reed stresses it. But bending oneself to a different shape is still just flexing; it does not usually result in a true change. You need to know what your "straight-up" condition looks like. Then you can bend at will within reason, and hopefully without cracking. You will still need to get "straight up" some times to minimize and relieve ongoing stress. Or you will even- tually crack and break.

So trying to achieve all the time definitely put my melancholy side on overload plenty of times and also set me up for emotional roller-coaster rides. My depression arises out of toxic mixes of all this. If I work too hard, I burn myself out physically and exhaust myself mentally and emotionally. Depression. If I don't work hard enough and feel I'm not "doing" anything or accomplishing things, I get down on myself. Depression. When I try so hard to make positive changes or help people, and get ugly, negative responses, I keep trying harder until I burn myself out trying and then I am just spent. Depression. If I get too busy and my living areas—office, house, and car—get too messy and out of order: depression. I am sure many can relate.

This dynamic was in force very early in my life. I tried hard to please my dad, but he never seemed pleased. I figured out later that that was one of the key strategies he used to drive us to be better. He used teasing the same way. It did drive me to be better, but it left me feeling like a flawed person or a failure a lot of times. I generally felt rejected. Of course, he was rarely happy himself, but I would read all of it as displeasure with me, personally. In hindsight, it obviously was never really about me at all, but as a child, everything is about you as far as you are concerned.

My mom got sick and I tried to help. She died anyway. I tried to be funny and be big and please my older siblings. It never seemed to work. I am sure I was obnoxious and hard to deal with at times, and of course, older siblings get annoyed with younger ones. As adults, several of my siblings have told me they thought I was funny, smart, and cute, but back then, as best as I can remember, I felt that they thought the opposite. All those roads led to a sense of rejection and failure. And to depression and despair.

My melancholy personality set me up for that, though. I thought so much and felt so much that I regularly went on emotional overload. A young child, and especially a boy, has enough problems processing feelings anyway, so overload is not hard to achieve. I was bright, aware, and in many ways mature beyond my years. I became a fixer and a problem-solver. From early on, I would work in the background to try to settle disputes and fix problems. There was nothing I would not give to help my family. I was generous with my things and later with my money. I don't think my family was even aware of all the different things I tried to do, at such a young age, to try to bless them and make our family work. I was very thoughtful and deliberate in it. Perhaps my motives were only selfish and designed to survive, but I do not really think so. I developed the heart of a minister early and remember sincerely caring about all those around me. It is one of life's consistent ironies, I believe, that our greatest challenges and even hurts create some of our greatest strengths.

My personality style, coupled with my life challenges, have certainly defined me. They also set the stage for a lifelong battle against depression. I have learned to control it, but the possibility of falling into depression is my ever-present companion, hiding in the caverns of my mind and heart.

However, being melancholy, I have stored up a wealth of knowledge and wisdom about people. I have studied and observed them. Being scientific, I have analyzed and categorized the information and experiences. Others are often surprised by the things I remember them having shared with me along the way. Being a driver or doer, I am also one to try to affect change. I am a reformer by nature. I am not satisfied with mediocrity or worse. I have constantly told my kids, "We don't do normal." I taught them that because I know what "normal" looks like, and frankly, I don't think it is a very good state of life. ("Normal" is an expression I have long used to describe what most would likely see as normal or average kinds of behaviors.) I should also state here that not ever feeling very normal has also been a source of pain for me along the way, as I have observed the lives of so many that were uncluttered and unfettered by the kind of troubling life challenges I have faced.

In addition, I am quite assertive. Others either tend to like me or not like me. There is very little in between. I have made some enemies with my convictions and the stands that I take. I am not much of a conformer, and that is costly when others try to force me to conform to some pattern they desire for me. Sometimes the cost of others' friendships or their approval is just too high for me. My dad always taught us not to be "followers." He had a cruder way of putting it, but he definitely drove that home to us.

Also, I am a change agent. I have spent my life trying to bring about positive changes. I am a pain in the neck to traditional conservatives—religiously and socially—because conservatives mostly oppose change. Maintaining status quo and minimizing change works for the "satisfied" and even for the complacent who like it the way it is and has always been. I, however, believe in change because I believe that the status quo is always shackled with shortcomings and is too often unjust toward the have-nots. Simply maintaining status quo also inherently produces endemic mediocrity. I do have a liberal heart in some ways—although not morally—but I try not to be governed by my own nature and personal preferences either way. I believe that Christ showed us and taught us the proper balance between maintaining what is right versus working to make changes in the things that are not.

I can be a pain in the neck to liberals, too, because I don't think all change is good. I do not think it is always "cool" to be accepting of certain human behaviors, moral shortfalls, laziness, and the like. I believe in God, the Bible, and right and wrong. My beliefs and convictions are not blind and are generally quite well considered.

So suffice it to say that my melancholy personality is one of my own depression challenges. As I previously mentioned, there are great books on the subject of personality and temperament that can prove help-ful in understanding susceptibility to depression. There is a wealth of information at your fingertips on the Internet. There are different kinds of assessments you can take for free or for a nominal charge that can help you understand yourself better. You are impor-tant. Take the time to understand the "car you are driv-ing," so to speak. Know yourself.

Chapter 7
Some Biblical Perspectives

Trust in the LORD with all your heart and lean not
on your own understanding;
In all your ways acknowledge him, and he will
make your paths straight.
(Proverbs 3:5-6)

My personal fight has been intense, and I have suffered greatly at Satan's hands. I have lost far too many battles. But I have not lost the war. And I am confident that I will not! I know that I am "more than a conqueror through Him who loves me" (Rom. 8:37). I know that everything that happens and everything that I feel, including my own dark moments, work out for my own good, as well as for God's purposes (Rom. 8:28; Eph. 1:11). I know how to endure all hardship, including depression, as discipline rather than punishment (Heb. 12:7). I know I can handle whatever life challenges I might face (Phil. 4:13). I know to rejoice in my trials, including my more melancholy moments

(James 1:2-4). As the Native American saying goes, "All sunshine makes a desert." I know I need to force myself to be thankful, even in depression (1 Thess. 4:18). Some of my greatest thoughts and changes have come out of spates of depression. I know to think about the positive things in and around me rather than the negative ones (Phil. 4:8). The world around us offers an infinite number of blessings every day, if we will only reach out and accept them gracefully. And finally, I know that the ultimate purpose of my despair is to teach me to rely on God and not on myself (2 Cor. 1:8-9). God will, however, bring the comfort I need in due time (2 Cor. 1:3-4). I further have discovered that the ultimate victory over worldly pain and trouble is found in my faith in Christ (1 John 5:4-5). I do believe, though, that my scars continually give rise to doubt and skepticism. They, coupled with my skeptical, analytical mind, cause me to have to fight for faith of any kind, especially faith in an infinite God.

I do not believe depression itself is a sin. Depression is first an emotional state. Concerning the emotion of anger, Paul said, "In your anger, do not sin…" (Eph. 4:26). Anger itself is not the sin, however it clearly can lead to sin (James 1:20). The "heart" part of our brain is deceptive because it produces emotions, constructs, and paradigms based on the information it is fed (Jer. 17:9). "Garbage in, garbage out," as we all well know. Further, Paul goes on to say that we should handle our anger (emotions) quickly in order to, "not give the devil a foothold" (Eph. 4:27). Not dealing with our emotions, especially the negative ones, gives Satan a foothold in our hearts. A foothold will become a stronghold (2 Cor. 10:4) if we are not grounded in and obedient to Christ. If we deal with our emotions quickly, as the Bible teaches, however, a lot of the painful fallout will be significantly reduced.

So, I say, in your depression, do not sin. Depression is an emotional state—a mindset, even. As I said earlier, depression is a type of emotional weather that blows in. Sometimes it is simply situational—a response to negative situations and stimuli. This is normal and will usually subside on its own for most people, although situational depression can become protracted and chronic in those prone to it. There is, however, another more destructive depression that is chronic, but non-specific. It comes out of nowhere and sticks around for far too long. It also can even be associated with the manic episodes of bipolar disorder, which needs immediate professional attention. Very often there are specific triggers to all kinds of depression. We can discover them if we are honest with ourselves. Often we do not want to admit what triggers it, as it may seem trivial or even silly to us or to others.

But some of our great Biblical role models faced types of depression and pervasive sorrow. Isaiah noted, far before Jesus came to the world, that even Jesus would be "a man of sorrows and acquainted with grief" (Isa. 53:3, NASB). And when Jesus sweated blood, he was not faking. He was deeply troubled and had been, on and off, for his whole life, I suppose.

The sad question he uttered in one of his darkest moments on the cross—concerning why God was forsaking him—was certainly not rhetorical (Matt. 26:46). Frankly, I think Jesus was quite melancholy most of the time.

I can assure you that while there is something for everyone in Jesus' life and teaching, there is a special connection for the true melancholy. Consider: "Jesus withdrew often to lonely places to pray" (Luke 5:16); Jesus sat on a hill and lamented the plight of the Jews (Matt. 23:37-39); and in his last hours he said to the apostles, "My soul is overwhelmed with sorrow to the point of death" (Mk. 14:34). At eleven years of age, he was talking to the religious leaders rather than playing kid games with the others at the Jerusalem celebration. Truly melancholic people understand and relate to all of that. I have deeply related to Jesus from those first days in college when I began to read the Gospels. His words and his life just speak so deeply and personally to me!

Paul, too, understood despondency. For example, he described to the Corinthians one of his experiences, saying,

> We were under great pressure, far beyond our ability to endure, so that we despaired even of life. Indeed, in our hearts we felt the sentence of death. But this happened that we might not rely on ourselves but on God (2 Cor. 1:8-9).

This was not a death wish uttered during a destructive state of depression, but a reflection on a harsh situation that made him think he would rather be dead than alive (Phil. 1:21). In this and other instances, Paul certainly did not exemplify the mythical Christian ideal of some modern Christians—that if we will be good and give generously, we will be happy and rich all the time.

Elijah was arguably the greatest of the Old Testament prophets. His was an unusual calling. First, he was sent to live alone by a stream and be fed by ravens. Yuk! Then, of all things, the stream dried up. Such seems to be the luck of melancholy people. ("God, you told me to go live by this stream and I did and you let the stream dry up! Why is that?") Then God sends Elijah to be taken care of by a pitiful widow who was preparing the last meal for herself and her starving son. That's depressing, too. ("Oh great, now I get to go mooch off a starving widow! Don't you know any rich people?") After all that, her son dies and she blames Elijah. In desperation, Elijah falls on the boy, begging God to raise him, and thankfully, God does just that (1 Kings 17:17-24).

Those trials and tribulations were only a prelude for Elijah's real battle with two of the most evil leaders ever, Ahab and Jezebel. He, of course, wins a major victory over their false prophets of Baal, executing all of them. Then, under the threat of execution himself, Elijah fears for his life and runs. Imagine that: he had just experienced a great miracle from God before the people. He had also personally led in the execution of hundreds of false prophets, which by the way, might have helped trigger his depression. But how could someone like Elijah be afraid of anything after that? Well, he was obviously a melancholy person.

In the flight for his life, he finally hides out in the desert. He sits down under a tree and says to God, "I have had enough, Lord. Take my life; I am no better than my ancestors." Then, in the typical fashion of one depressed, he falls asleep (1 Kings 19:4-6). So, if you have been thinking you are pretty useless and that God cannot use you because you get depressed, think again. Elijah can testify to the fact that God can and will use you, if you will just allow him. Even your darkness. If you want more on this, go read Elijah's whole story in 1 Kings 17 – 2 Kings 2. Paul himself learned the lesson that God actually glorifies himself in our weaknesses (2 Cor. 12:9-10).

Jeremiah was obviously melancholy. Gosh, he wrote a book they named "Lamentations"! God needed someone who could deal with the "dark side" to do what Jeremiah would have to do. He was "privileged" to foretell the final doom of the original nation of Judah. Boy, was he popular. Right. Listen to what this man of God had to say in his despair.

Oh Lord, you deceived me, and I was deceived; you overpowered me and prevailed. I am ridiculed all day long; everyone mocks me. Whenever I speak, I cry out proclaiming violence and destruction. So the word of the Lord has brought me insult and reproach all day long (Jer. 20:7-8).

He was not exactly mega-church preacher material. He would not be allowed on most religious broadcasts today. And he was not through with that depressing thought, either.

Cursed be the day I was born! May the day my mother bore me not be blessed! Cursed be the man who brought my father the news, who made him very glad, saying, 'A child is born to you—a son!' (Jeremiah 20:14-15).

Wow! He was not very happy, was he? But still, after all that, God kept on using him! I am not sure very many people could have gotten away with saying something like that to God. But Jeremiah just continued on with his depressing message. That was in fact his calling from God. Think about it—God made you and perhaps he wants you to use your melancholy personality to accomplish his purposes for you.

So, you see depression flows out of our emotions. Since the Bible reveals God's early interactions with man, you would expect to see the realities of depression in the lives of those mentioned. You do. There is certainly more there in each story. Much more. In fact, you see the whole range of emotions in the stories of the Bible. In the life of King David, you see psalms of joy (Psalm 9) and psalms of defeat (Psalm 51). You see in David a man who had the highest of highs, and you see in him a man who knew the darkness of deep depression. Peter, no doubt, fell into depression after his embarrassing denial of Christ just before Jesus' execution. He clearly lost confidence and hope. He withdrew and went back to fishing. It took a special visit by the resurrected Christ to restore Peter's hope.

So, armed with these thoughts, what is the Christian approach to sadness, despair, and depression? As with all human maladies, both physical and emotional, many of the so-called Christian solutions offered in the recent past were, to use Paul's expression, "no Gospel at all!" (Gal. 1:7). Trust me, I know. The church has, in the past, been pretty silent on the issue, often failing to recognize the ubiquitous nature of depression in modern society. Many and perhaps most Christians learned to repress and hide their depression. I think the church's sometimes misguided approach to life has probably actually triggered depression for many! It is as if we are to just give the command, "Rejoice in the Lord always" (Phil. 4:4). And that will fix it. If someone does not "get it," then the church just yells the command louder. They must not have heard or otherwise they have hard hearts. Or, we can live such stoic, joyless, and legalistic lives that depression is the expected pattern for Christians. Perhaps these are well-meaning teachings, but they are misguided for sure.

So, Christians are supposed to be "happy" all the time, are they not? Well, actually, maybe not. Really, no. Our role model was in fact a man of sorrow. Further, the first two of his now famous beatitudes are, "Blessed are the poor in spirit..." and "Blessed are those that mourn..." (Matt. 5:3-4). Perhaps we need to take a deeper and a fresh Biblical look at the subject of depression and examine all of the applicable commands through the lens of Jesus. Rather than simply applying a human interpretation to texts taken out of the greater Biblical context, we should view them in the context of the spirit and purpose of God himself.

Chapter 8
Is It Wrong for Christians to Use Antidepressants?

Darkness, clouds, and fog
Cover my head,
Shrouded over
By a pall of dread.

Sunshine and blue skies
Hide and disappear,
And hopes grow murky
And feelings drear.

Hazy air to fly through,
A dark day to weather,
Hurt unavoided,
Tomorrow will be no better.

    The Scripture does not run from the subject of depression. It actually gives a good prescription for a sound spiritual, mental, and emotional approach to it. The Bible also helps us understand realistic expectations for our existence. This world is not our home. Our hope is not in this world. The idea that we ought to be "happy" every minute of every day is not its reality or promise. Man apart from God must grab for it all here because it is all he has got. He must seek to make this life his "heaven."

For the believer, however, heaven is not yet. We see ourselves as visitors here in this present existence. We are strangers here, but we do have a mission though—"he [Jesus] died so that those who live would no longer live for themselves, but for him who for their sake died and was raised" (2 Cor. 5:15). We live for him. He designed a life for us. He wrote the book on it, and he perfected it for us (Heb. 12:2). Since we live for him, we "feel" for him. And he was a man "acquainted with sorrow." Hence, we must feel his sorrow for a little while. "Blessed are those that mourn, for they shall be comforted" (Matt. 5:4). "Grieve, mourn and wail. Change your laughter to mourning and your joy to gloom" (James 4:9). So, understand that for the Christian, not every episode of sorrow or melancholy is necessarily a destructive, chronic bout of depression to be remedied. It may well be a proper and necessary response. It may be God's will for us to suffer as it was his will for Christ: "Yet it was the Lord's will to crush him and cause him to suffer" (Isa. 53:10). A reality check, for sure!

Mental healthcare professionals generally diagnose serious chronic depression based on the presence of persistent symptoms over a certain time period, usually a couple of weeks. These include but are not limited to sleeplessness, irritability, fatigue, rapid changes in appetite, hopelessness, helplessness, self-hatred, feelings of worthlessness, inactivity, loss of interest in regular activities, and thoughts of suicide. It is unwise for any of us to unilaterally diagnose such serious mental health issues as depression in ourselves or in others. We must especially be cautious with regard to self-treatment. Rather, we need to consult with those who love us as well as others who are knowledgeable and trained. Watch out. There's a cottage industry feeding off the depressed as well as off those who are suffering other human maladies.

It is always best to see a reputable, trained professional to get insight and direction. If you are a Christian, go to see a Christian counselor or pastor. And do not stop seeking help until you have found a person who seems to know what he/she is doing. Not everyone who should understand it really does! Your family doctor might just be the first and best place to begin as she/he will be most familiar with your particular situation and can screen for underlying physical conditions that may be causing or aggravating your feelings of depression. Many medications can trigger or aggravate depression symptoms. There are many Christian doctors out there who can also help you think through some of the spiritual implications of certain medications and treatments. Your doctor might want you to try antidepressants or other medications in conjunction with counseling. In my reading and study, the prevailing thinking is that in serious depression, the best results are usually attained through a combination of short- or long-term drug therapy coupled with counseling therapy and lifestyle changes.

I must admit, however, that some in the church resist and often criticize the use of antidepressants. I beg to differ with many of their protests. Paul told Timothy to use wine to treat a stomach ailment and other illnesses when he could have told Timothy that he needed to pray more faithfully, or trust God more, or just let the Apostle Paul heal him (1 Tim. 5:23)! Jesus himself granted that the sick need a doctor. In fact, he even said this in spite of the fact that it was during a time when knowledge was limited and medical care could itself cause great harm (Matt. 9:12). In his illustrative story of loving one's neighbor, Jesus tells us that the loving Samaritan poured oil and wine on an injured man's wounds (Luke 10:27-37). I don't believe he would have used such examples or made these kinds of statements if seeing a doctor or using "medicines" were acts of unfaithfulness, weakness, or sin. Instead, he used this story as an example of doing good. Jesus is the creator (Col. 1:16) and as such, he told mankind to subdue (rule over) the earth (Gen. 1:28). When Hezekiah had a near-death experience, it was God who instructed him to use a fig poultice to treat a deadly boil. Hezekiah obeyed God and used the medicine, and, of course, still gave God the credit for healing him (2 Kings 20:1-11). The apostles did not seem to be bothered that Luke was a physician, and Luke did not give up medicine when he became a disciple.

Even before Christ, Hippocrates was prescribing a certain tree bark for pain and fever. It contained a substance called salicin, which is similar to aspirin (acetylsalicylic acid). Such helpful remedies for pain were certainly not unknown. Man started out as an intelligent, image-bearing species from the very beginning and anthropology and history has well documented this fact.

In fact, in "ruling over the earth," throughout history mankind has used many substances and remedies for medicinal purposes. Granted, substances have certainly been misused by men, as have many other parts of the creation. But using medicine is not unlike using certain foods, such as chicken soup and/ or herbs, to aid in healing and health. I simply do not believe taking action based on human learning is in any way unfaithful to God. Rather, I think it is a testimony to God's power in his children, who are made in his image and to whom he entrusted the use and care of his earth. God designed us as free beings with responsibilities and choices, not as string puppets that are under the constant threat of his wrath if we take action to help ourselves based on common sense and human learning. In my opinion, daring to take action based on our God given intelligence is often much more faithful than not doing so (James 2:14-26)!

It should be noted that James said that if we were sick we ought to call the elders and have them pray over us while anointing us with oil (James 5:13-16). This is, no doubt, an important Christian command and practice, which I heartily recommend. The anointing of oil, along with prayer, seemed to James to be important and well worth mentioning. And we should remember that James was led by the all-powerful Holy Spirit to write his letter. So, the point is not that the importance of faith and the work of God in healing must be diminished, but that God expects us to act in our own defense and for our own well-being. To take action based on our wisdom and knowledge can, in fact, be at least as trusting, if not more so, than simply sitting idly and expecting God to just give us whatever we desire. Give God the glory either way, as all good gifts come from him, however they happen to arrive (James 1:17). But take action! You are not helpless!

Jesus asked a long-term paralytic if he WANTED to get well (John 5:6). Are you kidding me?! Heck, yeah! Really, do you want to be well? Are you totally prepared for the responsibility of wellness? Are you truly desirous and prepared to leave your debilitation behind? There are significant "advantages" to be relinquished, you must know, if you decide to give up, your depression. At first glance, it seems the answer ought to be obvious. But for many of us there is a lingering codependence to, and perverted enjoyment of, our diseases. They can even give us a kind of power over others and even the illusion of strength and power within ourselves. Acting helpless can force those around us to take care of us. Being pitiful can minimize any expectations others have of us.

It is all a lie, however. You know, deep down, that it is. The net gain/loss between any elusive advantages and the constant disadvantages of being depressed is extremely net negative.

Chapter 9
Fighting and Beating Depression

Lying helplessly in darkness,
Longing for glimmer of light,
But none was forthcoming,
In blackness of night.

Standing against hopelessness,
Limping in fear into day,
Finding help and relief in learning,
To live by living for just today.

If your depression is sporadic and generally manageable, the following suggestions can go a long way in helping you achieve the kind of peace you want. Even if your depression is much worse, these strategies can be used in conjunction with other therapies you might be considering or are already utilizing, including medication. I have gleaned these ideas over the years from my own personal experiences as well as those of the seemingly hundreds of Christians I have known personally who faced depression and those whom I have counseled for it.

While I have considerable awareness of secular counseling techniques, my counseling is biblical and pastoral in nature and addresses the mental, physical, and emotional issues in conjunction with spiritual principles. I sometimes refer the more serious, chronic cases to other trusted professionals for medical treatment or for more advanced therapeutic approaches, while I continue to assist those individuals with my own biblical counseling and lifestyle management techniques. For Christians, I am a strong believer in working with counselors who are believers, as there often are inherent contradictions between secular counseling and spiritual and biblical principles. So with that said, here are my thoughts.

Adjust Your Expectations

First, change your expectations. I find that depression is often associated with unrealistic and/or unfulfilled expectations. The "American dream" is not all that dreamy anyway. Sometimes modern Christians believe that if one "gives it all to God" (especially one's money via a particular church or ministry) all will be wonderful. Now test that idea against our model of

Christianity, Jesus himself. In reality, this concept is unrealistic and even counter to what we see in Christ's own exemplary experience. Such promises do attract a lot more people to a church, though. However, this world is not heaven and we must not expect to be "happy" every moment of every day. Some sorrow is a part of a healthy, realistic life. We should strive instead to have constant joy, which is a much deeper virtue than just being happy. Joy is an outgrowth of faith in God that it will all turn out well and that our pain has a good purpose.

The melancholy personality carries a dark side, but some of the greatest human ideas have come from it, as well. The fact is, reality is not always pretty and needing to be "high" all the time leads individuals to all sorts of gimmicks to try to achieve it—even to the point of misusing drugs, alcohol, sex, and other things. Real life in Christ certainly won't keep you high all the time, but it will bring you the most joy possible. Consider the complete "Serenity Prayer" by Reinhold Niebuhr. Niebuhr was a well-known American theologian of German descent. Niebuhr strongly protested the utopianism proposed by early twentieth-century liberals. His writings on Realism remain influential throughout America as well as in other parts of the world. You will recognize the first few lines of the prayer, primarily because of its use by Alcoholics Anonymous and other recovery programs.

"The Serenity Prayer"

GOD, grant me the serenity
to accept the things
I cannot change,
Courage to change the
things I can, and
And the
wisdom to know the difference.
Living ONE DAY AT A TIME;
Enjoying one moment at a time;
Accepting hardship as the pathway to peace.
Taking, as He did, this
sinful world as it is,
Not as I would have it.
Trusting that He will make
all things right if I
surrender to His Will;
That I may be reasonably happy
in this life,
And supremely
happy with Him forever in the next.
Amen
(by Reinhold Niebuhr)

The prayer was popularized during World War II, an era of tremendous hardship and insecurity. Notice again some of his words: "Living one day at a time. Enjoying one moment at a time; Accepting hardship as the pathway to peace. Taking, as He did, this sinful world as it is, not as I would have it…that I may be reasonably happy in this life, and supremely happy with Him forever in the next."

That I may be reasonably happy. Too many of us, in our rightful longing for a blissful life, try to find a constant high through a perpetual but misguided search. Or, we attempt to fabricate it through our own devices. Neither is possible in this life. Trying to make the world around me be the way I want it is the ultimate prescription for frustration, disappointment, and depression for those prone to depression. Acceptance of the things I cannot change is essential to dealing with and healing from depression.

In our modern world, movies and marketing often send very unrealistic—and thus unhealthy— signals to the unsuspecting and naïve. I am encountering more and more individuals who fall prey to simply being disappointed with life. I find young men and women who have in their minds some ideal of a mate, but who will likely never find anyone even close to it because the mental "ideal" is just not realistic. I find so many who get to where they were trying to go in terms of education and career, only to find out that it is not making them happy. Many young people pursue fulfillment through popularity, relationships, sports, money, careers, and other life situations, only to find out it is just not there! To truly self-actualize we must deal with reality, not fantasy.

God said, "Why spend money on what is not bread, and your labor on what does not satisfy? Listen, listen to me, and eat what is good, and your soul will delight in the richest of fare. Give ear and come to me; hear me, that your soul may live" (Isa. 55:2-3). Too many people spend far too much on far too little and end up far away from where they want to be! Figure that out and you've got it. Paul said, "Do not think of yourself more highly than you ought, but rather think of yourself with sober judgment…" (Rom. 12:3). Don't think more highly of yourself than you ought. But don't think too little, either. Be realistic. Be sober (sane and logical) about your self-image.

Much attention has been given to the recent rise in the incidence of depression in society. Some or even a lot of that is likely due to simple recognition and reporting. However, I believe much of it is associated with modern expectations. Previous generations were not nearly as laden as we are with unrealistic expectations for life. Thus, they were not nearly as disappointed with life, an issue I believe to be one of depression's great triggers. Undoubtedly, high social and lifestyle expectations have brought about great inventions, innovations, and life improvements for the masses. However, what is the worth of these if the results do not bring greater contentment? I strongly believe that success is contentment, and contentment is success.

Maximize Your Strengths

If you are truly a melancholy personality, turn your personality into strength. As I have said, I have long observed that one's greatest strengths are also one's greatest weaknesses. Conversely, in our weaknesses we often find sources of untold strength! For sure, being melancholy presents inherent weaknesses. However, it also paves the way to the recognition of some great corresponding strengths. Some of the greatest leaders, thinkers, artists, and innovators in the world were or still are quite melancholy, Abraham Lincoln being one of the best known. The melancholy mindset brings a certain kind of seriousness as well as a reality-focus. The melancholy mindset brings mental storms that must be settled, and their settling often brings better understanding and ultimately many solutions or better approaches to individual and/or social problems.

Get off the Fence on Christ

Third, make a decision about Christ or God in general. Decide what you believe. Decide on what or in whom you will place your faith. Straddling the fence is awkward and frustrating. Many Christians try to live half in the world and half in Christ. Many who do not espouse Christianity or any religion live rather in doubt and skepticism. This is not good, especially for those who battle depression. Living in doubt is ultimately impossible. This duplicity brings frustration and, for those predisposed to it, depression. In such cases, people have enough of Christ to not completely enjoy the world anymore, but not enough to find the true underlying joy of being in Christ. It was Elijah who challenged the Israelites about their attempts to serve both God and the idol Baal, saying, "How long will you waver between two opinions? If the Lord is God, follow him; but if Baal is God, follow him" (1 Kings 18:21). Jesus said,

> No one can serve two masters. Either he will hate the one and love the other, or he will be devoted to the one and despise the other. You cannot serve both God and money (Matt. 6:24).

In this statement, "money" is symbolic of all the wrong worldly purposes contending with the right spiritual ones. You simply cannot serve both Christ and the purposes of this world, as they are opposites. This prolonged sense of frustration will be very troubling and even depressing. Jesus said it himself—be hot or cold about it, but don't get stuck in the middle (Rev. 3:15). You just have to choose.

Treat Your Body as a Temple

Take care of your body. To take care of our hearts and minds, we must first take care of the place where these reside and out of which they flow. We are made in God's image—body, soul, and spirit. For Christians, our bodies are also the temples of the Holy Spirit himself (1 Cor. 6:19). Be a good temple custodian! I said it was a temple of God's Spirit though, not our own idol; so don't obsess over your looks and physical perfection, etc. Get the proper amount of rest. When I finally discovered that extreme fatigue was one of my most significant triggers and took action to manage it, I eliminated a lot of my depression. Seems too simple, does it not?

Also, learn to manage stress. Get exercise of some kind. Exercise doesn't need to be all that vigorous, and in fact, less strenuous exercise might even prove more helpful. Just walk, for crying out loud! Exercise helps not only the body, but the mind as well. Soak up some sunshine. The power of the outdoors is incredible in its positive impact on our bodies, minds, and spirits.

Manage your work schedule. Have a purpose in life that is greater than simply working. Work to accomplish that greater purpose. Never let employment become an end unto itself, or else you submit yourself to human slavery. Working like this is sure to disappoint you.

Don't overload yourself. Multitasking is fine to a degree, but many get addicted to the adrenaline rush of it and burn themselves out. Contrary to many workplace cultures, harried is not a good thing, and in the end harried people and workaholics do not get more done.

Treat your underlying illnesses. Your body gets sick and breaks down sometimes. Take the time and make the effort necessary to get well. Trying to run on fumes will burn you out, and if you are depression-prone, it will throw you deep in the hole.

Each of these suggestions warrants a longer discussion, and there is a plenty of science behind each. I can tell you for sure that when I start feeling down, the first thing I try to do is take a nap or just get some rest. I used to try to get by on just a few hours of sleep a night, and I would simply wear down. At some point I would shut down, too. I've learned to take much better care of myself over the years—and I have greatly enjoyed the results!

Resolve Conflicts

It takes a heavy toll on us when we harbor the animosity, anxiety, and the anger involved in conflict. Learn to deal effectively with conflict. Paul said, "In your anger do not sin: Do not let the sun go down while you are still angry, and do not give the devil a foothold" (Eph. 4:26). You get that? Unresolved anger, like other troubling emotions, will give the devil a foothold in your life. He is the prince of darkness. No wonder our inner being becomes dark, as it is in depression, when he gains a foothold in us. Did you also catch what Paul said about dealing with your anger daily? Doing so is critical. Get better rather than bitter.

Jesus said, "Settle matters quickly with your adversary" (Matt. 5:25). Manage your conflicts and do it quickly. If you are harboring bitterness and "unforgiveness" toward others, forgive them for your own sake, and for God's sake, even if you think they do not "deserve" it. Then, start dealing with all your "stuff" daily, rather than letting it fester.

Take Action on Your Worries

Worry infects. Fix the problem. Change the attitude. Right-size the expectations; don't supersize them! Jesus said, "Do not worry about your life" (Matt. 6:25). Paul said, "Do not be anxious about anything…" (Phil. 4:6). To really do this, you have to first trust God to take care of you. This does not mean that God will give you everything you want or think you ought to have. This means trusting that what he does give you is what you really need, even when it is hardship (Heb. 12:7). Paul said, "If we have food and clothing, we will be content with that" (1 Tim. 6:8). That's not true for most of us a lot of the time, and this causes us great angst. Focus on what you have, not on what you don't have; focus on what is, not what isn't.

God's promise is certain. "And we know that in all things God works for the good of those who love him, who have been called according to his purpose" (Rom. 8:28). That's why Paul goes on to say that in Christ we are MORE than conquerors through our relationships with Christ (Rom. 8:37). And God has given us the keys to contentment. In fact in my way of thinking, true success is contentment, and contentment is success. If you have learned to be content with where you are and what you have at any given time, you have learned the secret to real, lasting success (Phil. 4:8-13).

Mend Relationship Problems

Take care of marital and other family relationships. Many other seemingly oppressive life issues really mask underlying relationship problems. If you are having marital problems, sit down and try to iron them out as best you can with your mate. Get help from a reputable counselor or pastor, if necessary. Don't play silly mind games that are really just deceptive forms of manipulation. They are useless and frustrating and always ultimately yield bad results. Grow up.

I meet so many in the counseling room who are emotionally immature. If I may be so blunt, they are "big babies." Hey girl, put on your big girl panties.

Listen dude, man up. Simply tell the other person what you need, what you think and/or what works for you, without accusing or threatening or belittling him or her. Then be forgiving, patient, compassionate, and realistic. You will be amazed how well this will work, especially if you do not let weeks, months, or years of "junk" accumulate before you address it.

Keep your relational house in order and tidy, and it will never become a mess. Again, manage those expectations. No relationship is constantly ideal.

Cut the Self-Pity

Stop feeling sorry for yourself. Self-pity is a killer in so many ways. Self-pity is emotionally malignant! It really is the opposite of thankfulness. Notice the connections Paul makes in the following verse: "Be joyful always; pray continually; give thanks in all circumstances, for this is God's will for you in Christ Jesus" (1 Thess. 5:16-18). Joy. Prayer. Thankfulness. Take a dose and see how it makes you feel.

Note that in Isaiah 55:2, God asks why we spend money and labor on what is not food and does not satisfy. Ultimately in this same text, God tells us what the purpose of his word is in our lives:

> It [God's word] will not return to me empty, but will accomplish what I desire and achieve the purpose for which I sent it. **You**

will go out in joy and be led forth in peace;
the mountains and hills will burst into song
before you, and all the trees of the field will
clap their hands. Instead of the thornbush
will grow the pine tree, and instead of briers
the myrtle will grow (Isa. 55:11-13).

God desires us to have joy and peace! God sent
his word for us to have joy and peace! Knowing the
truth of God's word and striving to obey it is the secret
of life satisfaction. However, be careful of assuming
that every doctrine out there is really God's word. "Let
the buyer beware" when it comes to church doctrine.
Read the Bible and think for yourself. Be open-minded
and seek God rather than just religion.

Take Care of Friendships

Foster healthy friendships. I cannot stress this
enough. However, if you are depressive by nature,
do not seek out and hang out with other depressive
people all the time. You need to primarily spend time
with people who do not struggle with dark thoughts.
If upbeat friends cannot get you out of depression,
they will insist that you go get help. That's the kind of
friendships you need in order to effectively address
your depression. Other depressed friends may in fact
"enjoy the company" and have subconscious motives
for you not to get better. I am not suggesting that

you drop your friendships with people who deal with depression just as you do. But make sure you have plenty of friends who do not.

Do not allow your friendships with your fellow strugglers to become opportunities for each of you to unload toxic negativity every time you are together. Trust me, such sessions may seem compassionate and helpful, but they are counterproductive over the long haul. And with your "non-struggling" friends, try to let them lead the direction of your conversations, as they will not generally focus on depressing things. I believe thought processes are very contagious. Negativity is a thought process as much as it is a belief. Positive thinkers will have a very positive impact on you.

Serve Others

You can buy happiness, in a way. You do it by spending your money on others who desperately need it. There really is greater blessing in giving than in receiving, as Jesus said (Acts 20:35). You can also actually "achieve" happiness in a way—be "saved by works." You do it by serving others instead of yourself. Serving is the greatest single antidepressant I know of. Just be sure to serve those who really need help. Do it expecting nothing in return. Do it in secret as much as possible, so your reward will come from God himself (Matt. 6:2-4). There are many and varied opportunities for Christian service. Find one and work at it, especially when you are fighting to not get "down."

Take Strength from Christ

Get your deeper joy from the reality of Christ. Paul's words in Phil. 4:4-13 are, in my estimation, some of the most pertinent words in the whole Bible for spiritually addressing depression. At the end of this passage Paul says, "I can do everything through him who gives me strength" (v. 13). Now, it is easy to assume that Paul is talking about the power to conquer things and do things. It does sort of mean that in the bigger picture. But if you look at what he says just prior to this, you will see how it applies to depression. "I have learned the secret of being content in any and every situation…" (v. 12). He is discussing gaining the ability to be content whatever the circumstances. What did he learn that brought him contentment? Well, look further back in his logical progression,

> Finally, brothers, whatever is true, whatever is noble, whatever is right, whatever is pure, whatever is lovely, whatever is admirable— if anything is excellent or praiseworthy— think about such things. Whatever you have learned or received or heard from me, or seen in me—put it into practice. And the God of peace will be with you (Phil. 4:8-9).

Focus on things that are excellent and praise-worthy. Yes, it does take mental discipline. But put it into practice and you will get better at it.

Next, look back at the start of the Philippians text. "Rejoice in the Lord always…the Lord is near" (vv. 4-5). These verses are not about being "happy." They refer to the central thought from which you should get your deep inner joy. When one wants to feel real joy, one thinks about things that are precious or things to be looked forward to. However, here Paul is saying that you should think instead about what you have in the Lord. Rejoice in the Lord. Through Jesus, God demonstrated an incomparable and inconceivable love for each of us. "But God demonstrates his own love for us in this: While we were still sinners, Christ died for us" (Rom. 5:8). God demonstrated it—unconditional love. Because that is in fact his very essence (1 John 4:8). Our ultimate joy is what God desires. But you are not going get it from stuff in this world because the temporal will ultimately disappoint you every time.

I spend a lot of time processing that kind of disappointment with people. What we gain from the reality of the gospel, however, will never disappoint us. Just look at Rom. 5:5. "And hope does not disappoint us, because God has poured out his love into our hearts by the Holy Spirit, whom he has given us." This singular reality is the spiritual antidote to depressive thinking—the hope of God. (In the Bible, "hope" is not a "wish" as we think of it today, but rather it is an expectation—what we firmly believe will happen.) The reality is that with God, I am deeply and unconditionally loved, I am badly wanted, and I am richly blessed, so why go scavenging for any of it? If I get that, I can better accomplish what Paul commands next:

> Do not be anxious about anything, but in everything, by prayer and petition, with thanksgiving, present your requests to God. And the peace of God, which transcends all understanding, will guard your hearts and your minds in Christ Jesus" (Phil. 4:6-7).

The God of peace will guard your hearts and minds. Yes, you have to work at it. "Work out your salvation…" (Phil. 2:12). But in doing so, always remember: "It is God who works in you to will and to act according to his good purpose" (Phil 2:13).

Don't Give Up

Never give up. One of the most inspiring speeches ever given was by Winston Churchill. It was during World War II, October 29, 1941, at the Harrow School outside of London. Here is the most famous excerpt. I think it aptly applies to the fight against a foe as formidable as depression:

> This is the lesson: never give in, never give in, never, never, never, never—in nothing,

great or small, large or petty—never give in except to convictions of honour and good sense. Never yield to force; never yield to the apparently overwhelming might of the enemy.

You must never give in. You must never yield to "the apparently overwhelming might of the enemy." Churchill was referring to the incredible assault of the German army on Britain—indeed the attack being felt on the very area in which he was speaking. Great Britain, the United States, and the allies turned the tide and won this bitter world battle. Churchill's was arguably the voice of leadership in the ultimate defeat of one of the most frightening foes of humanity ever—Naziism!

His "never give up" attitude is also crucial to the defeat of this other dark foe of humanity—depression. It too will wreak havoc on the terrain of your heart and soul if you do not fight fiercely against it. In speaking of the ultimate destroyer, Satan, Jesus said, "The thief comes only to steal and kill and destroy" (John 10:10).

Never give in. You really can win this battle.

Chapter 10
How to Help a Friend or Loved One Deal with Depression

Reached out to a loved one sinking,
Saw in his eyes deep despair,
He reached back and grabbed me in panic,
His weight was more than I could bear.

A lot has been written about depression—both on how to recognize it and on how to deal with it in others. Suffice it to say, being around someone who is depressed is usually a chore; living with someone who is chronically depressed is burdensome. One of the great challenges of dealing with depression is the complicated social interactions it requires. I have eight suggestions for people who are coping with a depressed loved one.

In the long run, the first and most important thing you can do to help someone you love is to take care of yourself. If you think of depression as negative energy, you can understand how it can draw energy out of you—literally "suck the life" out of you. Sometimes you can deal with it by being at least as positive as the other is negative. However, it is unrealistic to expect yourself to be constantly "up." Also, you must not allow yourself to become codependent with one who is depressed. Codependency is a psychological condition in which we allow ourselves to be controlled to a large degree by the mood cycles of another. Codependency usually involves a high degree of manipulation, and depressed individuals often learn to manipulate those around them through their depression.

Make sure you have close contact with mentally healthy people. Relying on a depressed person as your sole support is a huge mistake. It's much like trying to save a drowning person by swimming to him face-to-face, rather than approaching from behind as recommended. If you swim right up to them, it is likely the person will grab you around your neck, hang on for dear life, and with his adrenaline-induced strength, drown you! A depressed person can certainly "drown" you in her/his darkness. You must not let a depressed person control or otherwise consistently manipulate you. Staying in close touch with a couple of other healthy individuals, especially those unattached to the depressed person, is essential to your own mental health. Hiding your loved one's depression will not help it go away; it will only enable it to become worse!

Empathize and even sympathize, but do not enable. Depression can often become an excuse to fail. It is often an excuse not even to try. Any individual has the choice to give in to depression or to fight it. Anyone who believes he or she doesn't have a choice believes a lie. If one is battling depression, then likely there's not a choice about its actual onset, but there IS a choice in whether to fight it or not. And there is a choice whether to give in to it or not. There are choices and there are options. You must not believe, and you must never enable a depressed person to believe, that he or she is hopeless and without options.

The reality is that we all ultimately have the option to self-destruct. You must not take on the responsibility of making or keeping another person healthy. You should communicate that you will help that person, but that you cannot do the work for him. Be firm without being stern in communicating with him. Do not allow yourself to feel guilty because you are not depressed, even if the depressed one expresses jealousy of your apparent mental health. It is NEVER your fault that someone else is depressed. Keep emphasizing that we have choices to fight depression or to yield to it. Encourage him or her to choose the mentally healthy option.

The second thing you can do is to educate yourself. The adage "knowledge is power" is true. The more you know, the more you can help. It will keep you from believing the lies a depressed person may believe. It will allow you to speak the truth to her/him.

Understanding that the propensity for depression is in one's DNA can help relieve both your guilt and the other's. It is equally important to understand that the choice of fighting and overcoming depression is not genetic. It is an act of one's will, and it is accomplished one baby step at a time.

Educating yourself will allow you to gauge the severity of a loved one's depression at any given time. Take seriously another's threats of suicide or otherwise harming herself. Talk about it. Don't be afraid to ask her if she is contemplating harming herself. Don't be afraid to discuss self-destructive behaviors with him. Suicide is often an impulsive act, but other harmful behaviors, such as alcohol and/or drug abuse, can be just as destructive over time. If any threat seems immediate, don't hesitate to call 911. For guidance on wise steps you can take, call a suicide hotline. They are manned by people who are trained how to talk to depressed individuals or to advise their loved ones.

The third thing is to urge the depressed person to get ongoing help and support. One can start down the path with a reputable counselor or pastor. I must say with all due respect, however, that not all counselors or pastors are good at dealing with depression. I have seen some counselors who seem more bent on keeping the person coming back than on helping him control depression. The approaches of these counselors, I believe, enable depression more than treat it. In addition, some pastors have bought into a belief that all depression is merely a choice and can thus simply be "un-chosen." It is odd to me that those who have been given the responsibility of administering the grace of Christ can at times be cold and harsh, lacking gentleness, in their approaches to real human maladies. I believe they are naïve or misguided, albeit likely sincerely so. At worst, they have bought into shallow, thoughtless, or insensitive Biblical interpretations that seem more predatory than benevolent.

Going to a psychiatrist as a first step will often lead to immediate medication, with or without encouragement to seek counseling therapy. In general, I believe pursuing drug therapy alone, or as a first treatment step, is unwise in the case of depression, and I think research bears that out. Education and support should come first so that the depressed individual can make wise choices with a measure of confidence.

A good counselor will help a depressed person chart a course of action that makes the most sense. A good counselor will give the depressed person hope for improvement. A good counselor will help the person evaluate the effectiveness of various treatments. The counselor also can help the depressed person to be more sensitive to needs of those around him.

One thing that will be necessary for committed Christians is to have good Biblical teaching and pastoral support. Many spiritual barriers have been erected in the hearts and minds of individuals and church communities concerning mental health. Many pastors have preached vociferously against the whole idea of mental health, usually scoffing at drug therapy for mental health. Many depressed Christians are convinced they are spiritually weak or immature, or they are just sinful people and if they can repent enough, their depression will subside. In reality, the whole Christian milieu is treacherous for those who are mentally or emotionally ill. Sadly, in my opinion, so is the secular mental-health system. However, finding communities that work with the depressed will lead to referrals to wise, supportive, and helpful counselors and pastors.

The fourth thing is to get your own counseling assistance if your loved one's depression is chronic and/or severe. This help can come from the same counselor or from another. This therapy probably does not need to be ongoing, but it can be, if necessary. It can help you evaluate whether you, too, have become depressed or if you have become codependent. It can help you to chart your own course of action. If you live with or are close to one who battles depression, you will likely experience any number of difficult emotions, including helplessness, frustration, anger, fear, and guilt. Acknowledging these understandable but ultimately damaging emotions is critical to uprooting them from your own psyche. A good counselor can help you to look sanely and helpfully at these common emotional reactions. Trying to help a depressed person by oneself is simply a big mistake. Depression can be very complicated even for one trained in it; it is nothing to play with for a nonprofessional. Get help for yourself.

Fifth, keep the lines of communication open. You will need to be creative in discussing it, but let it be known that if you are to maintain contact with the depressed person, you need to be able to discuss the problem. Treat depression as you would any physical illness in terms of checking in and seeing what is needed. Make sure the individual understands that the depression is indeed an illness, even if it is chronic, and that the mutual goal is healing and relief. A counselor can help you to develop specific approaches to open communication. But it is also healthy to make it clear that you will not support any course that would allow your loved one to wallow in self-pity or helplessness and not battle his malady.

Sixth, stay active. Physical and social activities are essential both for the depressed and for those living with them. Physical activity consistently has been shown to help one's attitude and sense of well-being. Social activities also provide wonderful opportunities to engage in healthy interactions that lead to healthy friendships, meet your own needs, and help you to build up emotional stamina. Also, striving to include a depressed person in activities can be a huge help to him. Simply getting him to take even short walks, especially in the sunshine, can be therapeutic for both of you. A consistent exercise program is a good course. Enrolling in a dance class, a fitness program, or an educational or social program can be very helpful. Support groups for those who are depressed and/or for those supporting a depressed person can prove pivotal in beating depression.

Seventh, turn to God. Pray for the other's healing. Speak the truth of God's word into her/his heart and life. For those of a Christian persuasion, it is essential to reconcile a healing course with scripture. A scripture I pointed out earlier as a favorite passage concerning how to turn to God with depression is Philippians 4:4-13.

> Rejoice in the Lord always. I will say it again: Rejoice! Let your gentleness be evident to all. The Lord is near. Do not be anxious about anything, but in every situation, by prayer and petition, with thanksgiving, present your requests to God. And the peace of God, which transcends all understanding, will guard your hearts and your minds in Christ Jesus.
>
> Finally, brothers and sisters, whatever is true, whatever is noble, whatever is right, whatever is pure, whatever is lovely, whatever is admirable—if anything is excellent or praiseworthy—think about such things. Whatever you have learned or received or heard from me, or seen in me—put it into practice. And the God of peace will be with you.
>
> I rejoiced greatly in the Lord that at last you renewed your concern for me. Indeed, you were concerned, but you

had no opportunity to show it. I am not saying this because I am in need, for I have learned to be content whatever the circumstances. I know what it is to be in need, and I know what it is to have plenty. I have learned the secret of being content in any and every situation, whether well fed or hungry, whether living in plenty or in want. I can do all this through him who gives me strength.

Paul's admonition is first for us to find our joy in the recognition of who Christ is, what he has already done for us, and what he will do for us if we will turn to him (v. 4). "Rejoice in the Lord!" Then react with gentleness (a lack of panic and fear) toward life's challenges and stresses, such as depression (v. 5). We are to lay our anxieties out to him in a thankful way (v. 6). His promise is that Christ's peace will "guard our hearts and minds" (v. 7). Further, he instructs us in positive thinking and outlook (v. 8). Paul then explains that the secret to contentment is found in this God-reliant attitude, concluding that with the right attitude, one can "do all things through Christ" (v. 13), or in other words, face with contentment whatever circumstances life may bring each of us. While the right attitude will not immediately heal chronic and perhaps physiologically induced depression, it will prime the depressed individual and those who love her for success.

Lastly, never, never, never give up. As I said previously, this admonition applies most aptly to the depressed individual. But it also applies to those who love him! A person who is depressed will greatly benefit from the resolve and faith of a friend or loved one. A kind, gentle strength and resolve flowing from a true friend can be the one factor that will ultimately lead a depressed person to a healing course.

Chapter 11
Conclusion

You do not have to live on in depression. Depression is an intergenerational double whammy: We often learn to live in depression from the ones from whom we inherited the propensity for it. We get a double dose. However, depression is not something you want to spread around. Depression is not something you want to pass on.

Early on, I drew a line in the sand and said I was not passing on to my children the junk that had unwittingly been passed on to me. To do that, however, I had to address it in my own life. To teach my own children new patterns of thought and action and to bless my wife with a mate who was not constantly depressed, I had to learn new patterns of living for myself. It has not been a cakewalk, and I have developed very realistic expectations. I have left no stone unturned.

Sadly, it took me far too long to try my last strategy, antidepressant medication, which finally given me needed biochemical relief while I concurrently apply all the other strategies. Medication was not my first approach though, and I do not think it should be for anybody. However, the best-tuned car will die if it has no gas in the tank. I was running on emotional fumes, so to speak, so much of the time—especially during my periods of dark depression. For me and for others, the right medication can be a life-saver. With good medical and mental-health supervision, there is no reason to be ashamed, and there is no reason to be afraid.

The one thing that makes the effort worth it is my relationship with God. By living in him, I have a deeper and more meaningful sense of purpose than I ever could have imagined. To me, this is not religious rhetoric. To me, it is real and experiential. To me, it is logical, not mythical. I have learned the secret of contentment. I have come to know the love that surpasses knowledge. I now experience the peace that passes understanding. He is the morning light for my dark days and he is the ultimate light for a dark world.

Never, never, never give up in your quest to manage and even conquer your depression. Life does not have to be lived in darkness and despair. There is a place in your own heart where there is day and there is joy. Go find it.

Quell my darkness and my doubt,
Still my inner being,
Calm the storm that rages within;
Keeps my heart from singing.

Your utter beauty and striking light,
Often seem untouchable; out of reach,

Some days all I can seem to do is fight,
Living in the breach.

Stop my worry and drive away my fear,
Strengthen my weak resolve.
Wash away my sin; remove my guilt,
All my hurt dissolve.

God, you are my healer,
I ever rely on you,
You guide me down a straight path,
In all I think and do!